DECODING STOCK MARKET

Acquire ! Apply ! Ascend !

--WRITTEN BY--

--Adithya Raj R--

Decoding Stock Market

Adithya Raj

How this book can work miracles in Your Life

I have seen miracles happen to men and women in all walks of life all over the world. Miracles will happen to you, when you Start believing it in you. This book is designed to teach you how to kick start your self in stock market with providing the right knowledge to get started with your plan of learning stocks

Do you know the answers?

Why is one man joyous and prosperous and another man poor and miserable? Why is one man fearful and anxious and another full of faith and confidence? Why does one man have a beautiful, luxurious home while another man lives out a meager existence in a slum? Why is one man a great success and another an abject failure? Why is one speaker outstanding and immensely popular and another mediocre and unpopular? Why is one man a genius in his work or profession while the other man toils and moils all his life without doing or accomplishing anything worthwhile? Why is one man healed of a so- called incurable disease and another isn't? Why is it so many good.

Reason for writing this book

 It is for the express purpose of answering and clarifying the above question and many others of a similar to nature that motivated me to write this book.I have endeavored to explain the great fundamental truths of stocks in simplest language possible. I believe that it is perfectly possible to explain the basics, foundation and fundamental of stocks. Special thanks to Investopedia, google and umar are the person who encoraged me to write the book .You will find the language of this book is used in ordinary everyday language . I urge you to study this book and apply the techniques outlined there in and as you do

Unique feature of this book

The unique feature of this book is its down-to-earth practicality. Here you are presented with simple, usable foundation and techniques. which you can easily apply in your workaday world.

--Path To Prosper--

CONTENTS

Hope you are interested in the stock market and want to invest your time in learning it.

This book will give you the right knowledge to get started with your plan of learning stocks

So let's get started!

Before getting started though,

What is Stock?

Stocks are an equity investment that represents part ownership in a corporation and entitles you to part of that corporation's earnings and assets. In the past, shareholders received a paper **stock** certificate — called a security — verifying the number of shares they owned.

What is Trading?

When you check the dictionary for the meaning of a **trader**, it says 'a person who buys and sells goods, currency, or shares'. So, in any market place, selling and buying are called **TRADE** and the people who do that are called **TRADERS**.

Different types of Assets in Trading:

Stock Trading

Option Trading

MCX Commodity Trading

Forex Trading

Stock Trading :

Stock trading refers to the buying and selling of **shares** in a particular company; if you own the **stock**, you own a piece of the company.

Option Trading:

An **option** is a contract that allows (but doesn't require) an investor to buy or sell an underlying instrument like a security, ETF or even index at a predetermined price over a certain time. Buying and selling **options** are done on the **options** market, which **trades** contracts based on securities.

MCX Commodity Trading:

Multi Commodity Exchange of India Ltd (**MCX**) is an independent **commodity** exchange based in India. ... **MCX** offers options **trading** in gold and futures **trading** in non-ferrous metals, bullion, energy, and several agricultural **commodities** (mentha oil, cardamom, crude palm oil, cotton, and others).

Forex Trading:

Forex, also known as **foreign exchange** or **FX trading**, is the conversion of one **currency** into another. It is one of the most actively **traded** markets in the world, with an average daily **trading** volume of $5 trillion.

--These are the main areas where you can make money from--

Each is a different market when compared to one another however these markets become the same under the Trading chart (The **trading chart** displays information that can help you decide when to enter and when to exit a position)

This chart helps you to enter the trade and exit the trade and at the end of that trade you will either be making your own cash flowing machine or you would lose the trade

--I will be helping you on getting started to make your device, a cash flowing machine--

--I am going to guide you through the basics and then expand on them as we go on--

Things to learn and never forget while Trading

The first thing you need to learn is how to control risk on the trade you have taken and not let the emotion drive you into a big fat loss. After that you can learn to be selective with your trading entries. Once you have mastered these things, you are one step ahead to build your own cash flowing machine

Let's move on to the basics

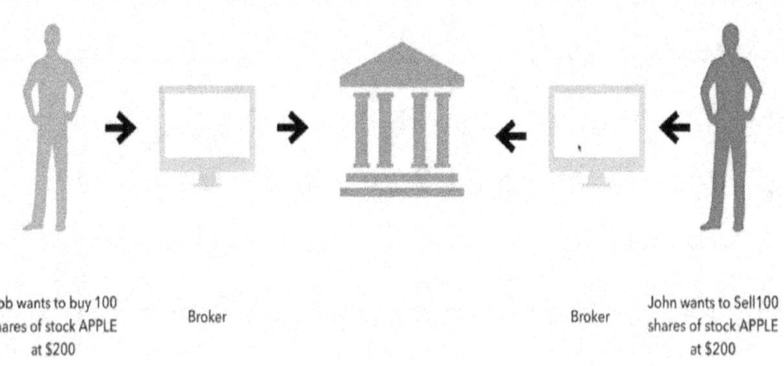

Here, Bob wants to buy apple stock at the price of 200, to do so he needs to go to the broker and when I say broker, it does not mean he should physically go to his broker. He can just go online and access websites like Zerodha, TD Ameritrade etc.,. They go to the market and check whether there is anyone who is willing to sell the apple stock at 200. By then, John gets in and he wants to sell the apple stock at 200 for 100 shares. Now the market exchanges the two parties to get the transaction done

So, It means that Bob gets the 100 shares for 200 and John gets the money for selling 100 shares for 200

Taking a closer look at brokers, they charge the commission for the process and it can vary from broker to broker.

Suppose Bob is willing to buy the share for 250 and John is selling for 200, will the transaction take place?

The answer is no, It won't take place. You can only buy a share at a price where there is a seller for that particular price.

Hope you're able to grasp the concept now. Let's move further.

What actually is a stock?

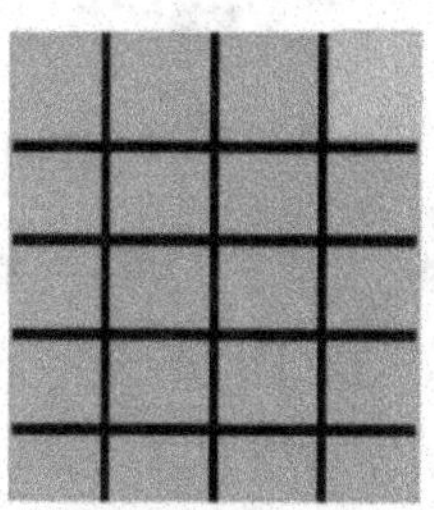

Stock is basically ownership in a company. Let's say the grid is a company called XYZ and it has a share of 20 shares in it and each share is for 5. In this case, the company is worth 100. Now if you want to buy the whole company u have to pay 100 to buy it. Let's say you buy **two shares** of the company XYZ which cost you 10 and if each share of the company goes up tomorrow to 6 from 5 you make a profit of 2 which means you have now 12 with you and the company grows to 120.

Each company has its own market department

For example, Apple's share is of 270 and let say Amazon's share is for 1500,you might say Amazon has a huge market department.

To conclude this assume that Apple has the share price of 270 and it has 100 shares and Amazon's share price is of 1500 and it only has 10 shares, I hope it is clear as an easy maths calculation will show you that Apple's market department is of 27000 whereas Amazon's market department is 15000.

The first thing a trader needs to learn is to become profitable and to control losses. If this was the only thing I could teach you it would at least give you 50/50 chance of becoming profitable. As far as I am reasoning, any trade must be proven right immediately or I shouldn't be in that position

Market moves in thrusts between implied support and resistance if we enter positions at the critical point the market will either agree with us or disagree with us.

To start with, market can do only three things :

GO UP or known as UPTREND

GO DOWN or known as DOWN TREND

GO SIDEWAYS, known as HORIZONTAL TREND

 UPTREND

An uptrend describes the price movement of a financial asset when the overall direction is upward. In an uptrend, each successive Peak and Through is higher than the ones found earlier in the trend. The uptrend is therefore composed of higher Swing highs and higher swing highs. As long as the price is making these higher swing lows and higher swing highs, the uptrend is considered intact. What you need to know is that a downtrend is composed of two types of price waves. They include:

- **Impulse**
- **Correction**

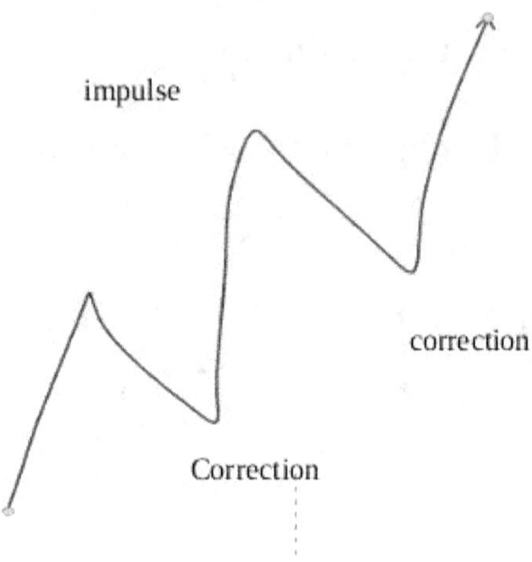

impulse
correction
Correction

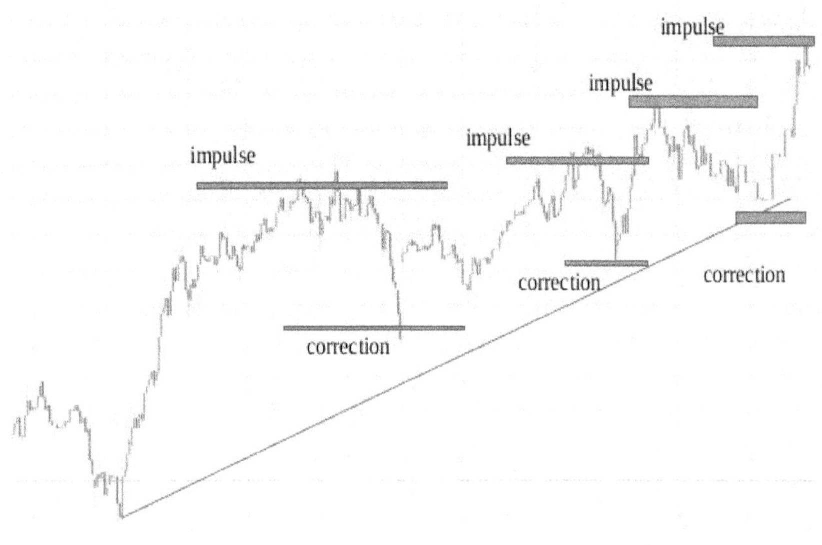

impulse
impulse
impulse
impulse
correction
correction
correction

DOWNTREND

A downtrend is when price action in a stock is moving lower over a period of time and is most recognizable by prices creating lower lows and lower highs.

Stocks in a downtrend continue in a trend down until certain market conditions change the direction. A downtrend is typically reversed by the supply of shares investors are planning on selling compared to the demand of investors who want to buy the stocks

What you need to know is that a downtrend is composed of two types of price waves. They include:

- **Impulse**
- **Correction**

correction
impulse

DOWNTREND

correction
correction
Impulse
impulse
impulse

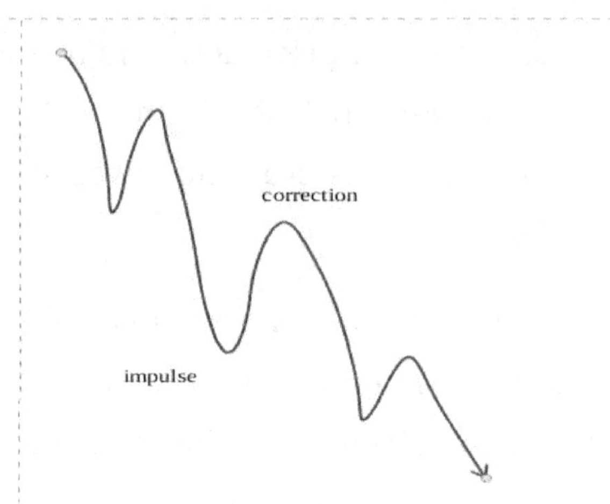

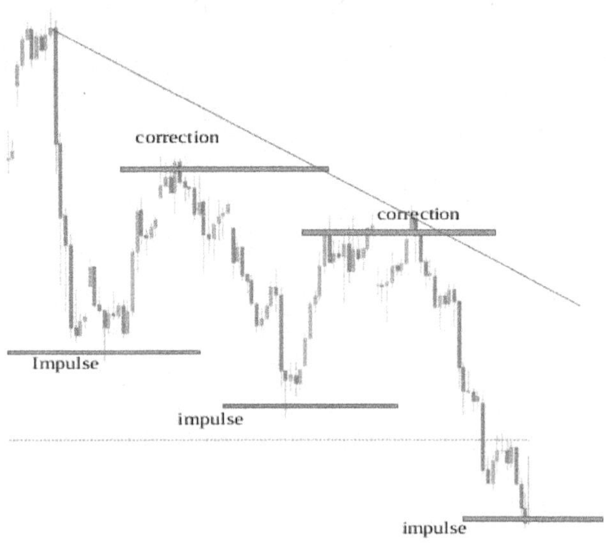

SIDEWAYS TREND

A sideways trend is the horizontal price movement that occurs when the forces of supply and demand are nearly equal. This typically occurs during a period of consolidation before the price continues a prior trend or reverses into a new trend . Sideways trends are generally the result of a price travelling between strong levels of support and resistance. It is not uncommon to see a horizontal trend dominate the price action of a specific asset for a prolonged period before starting a new trend higher or lower. These periods of consolidation are often needed during prolonged trends, as it is nearly impossible for such large price moves to sustain themselves over a longer-term.

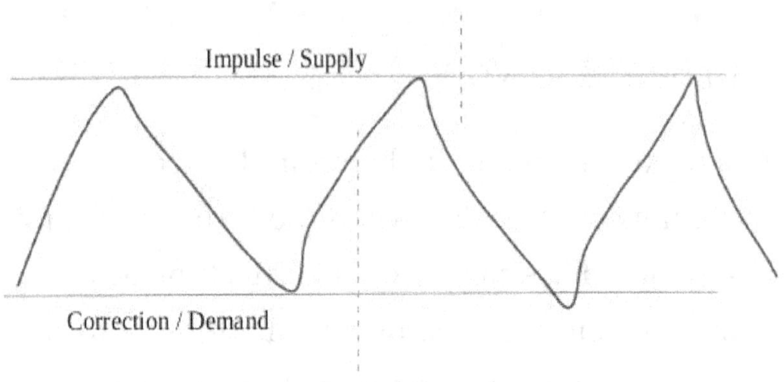

SIDE WAYS

Market never shows the same stuff that you have learned

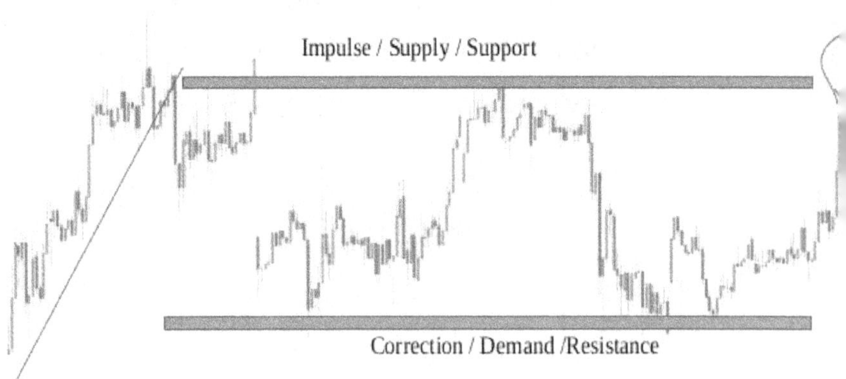

What happens in the above scenario is the demand takes out the supply zone and kicks it to a bullish trend

.   .   .

SUPPORT AND RESISTANCE

Support, resistance and Trend are the 3 most important issues for a professional trader.

SUPPORT:

This is the perceived level where buyers will return to the market and sellers will stop selling and begin to cover.

RESISTANCE:

This is the perceived level where buyers will stop buying and take profits and sellers will step up their selling activity.

When the market price reaches levels perceived, it will support or resist, it will demonstrate signs as the buying or selling dries up due to the increase in activity by the side that anticipates the level in advance.

Professional Traders generally have several methods for anticipating support or resistance levels in advance and will nest orders in the market before the price market reaches these levels

It really depends on how many orders are nested at these levels as to whether they actually turn out to become SUPPORT AND RESISTANCE

.   .   .

TREND

You will be hearing most of the time that TREND is your friend in your market and if you go against your friend you will lose your trade and your money as well.

It is said to be your friend because over time a trend will expand further allowing you opportunities to go with or go against when overbought or oversold

An example of uptrend

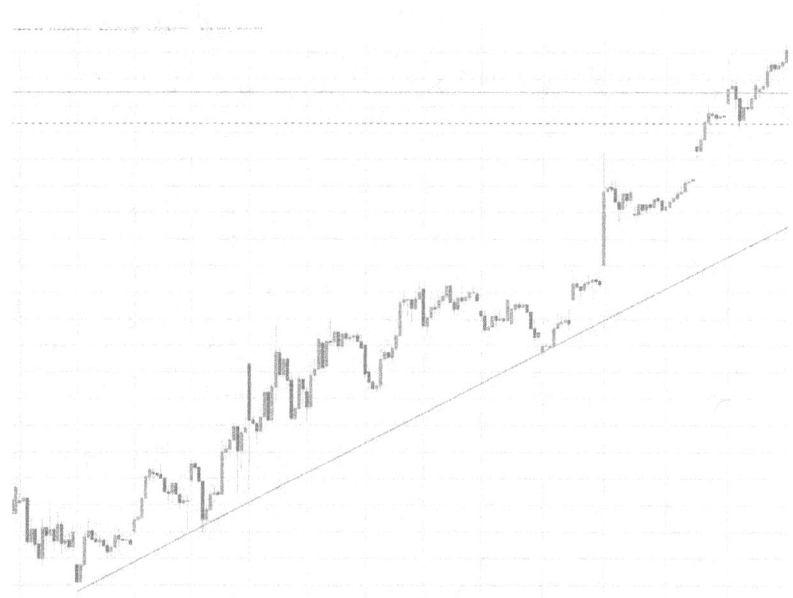

DownTrend

Once you understand how to deal with trend lines, its kind of like your friend is helping you make money constantly

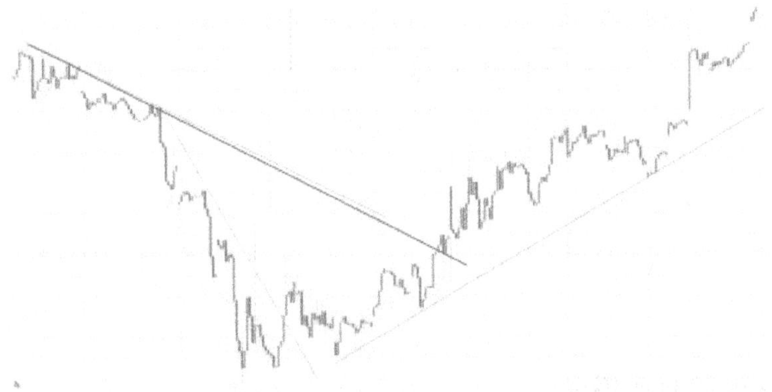

The above examples were broken into two to give you an understanding of trend . Above everything, you should know when and where the trend is going to break

The main thing when you are dealing with a trend line is that you should know when and where you can avoid losses and make profits into your pocket

With all aspects of it you should be wise in trading and take profits when you see the market in a move

--Future prediction in the market can get you in trouble--

What is Stock chart?

A chart is a graphical representation of price and volume movements of a stock over a certain time. In the graphical chart, the X-axis represents the time period and the Y-axis represents the price movement. The period can vary from intra-day to even a few months or more.

Ticker symbol, Time frame, charts, and volume

Ticker symbol

A **ticker symbol** or stock **symbol** is an abbreviation used to uniquely identify publicly traded shares of a particular stock in a stock market. A stock **symbol** may consist of letters, numbers or a combination of both.

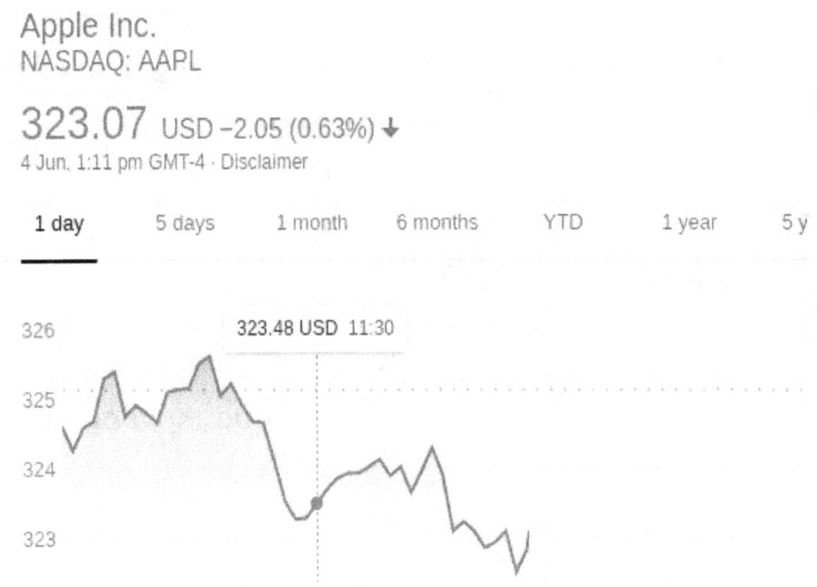

Apple Inc.
NASDAQ: AAPL

323.07 USD −2.05 (0.63%) ↓
4 Jun, 1:11 pm GMT-4 · Disclaimer

| 1 day | 5 days | 1 month | 6 months | YTD | 1 year | 5 y |

Time frame

Period:

When it comes to charts, the most popular time period for investors and swing traders is daily. This means that price information will be for one day. You can see how to set the periods below.

Common time period choices include

◆ Monthly
◆ Weekly
◆ Daily
◆ Hour
◆ Minutes
◆ Minute

Range:

Range displays how many periods you want to display, which is an important choice depending on the information you seek. Stock charts show quickly, without a lot of description, where price has been for a particular period of time. When you set the range, you know the stock's movement for that period of time.

Some default range settings are

◆ 1 day

◆ 5 days

◆ 10 days

◆ 1 month (roughly 22 trading days)

◆ 3 months (25 percent of a year, 63 trading days)

◆ 6 months (50 percent of a year, 129 trading days)

◆ 12 months (one year, 258 trading days)

◆ 3 years

◆ 5 years

◆ 10 years

◆ Year to Date

◆ Select Start/End Date

Traders or investors choose a time frame based on the type of decisions they want to make.

For example:

◆ Short-term traders select a three-month time frame most often because they plan to exit in the same day or within a few days. The three-month time frame gives them enough information to see the trend visually, but not too much information that can make it difficult to see an exit point. These charts can be intraday to describe what is happening for the day. Using a chart with five to ten days broken into one-hour candles can show a stock starting to improve or break down.

◆ Investors are less concerned with intraday movements and tend to select a one-year chart so they can catch longer trends. Because they will likely hold a stock for months or years, investors want to see how the stock has done over many years rather than just a few months. When they are trying to pick an entry or exit point, long-term investors will look to monthly charts.

◆ Institutional investors tend to use 20-year charts with monthly time frames, but they will look at many different time frames as they make decisions for their portfolios.

Price change

Which is also known as (OHLC)

Bullish candle:

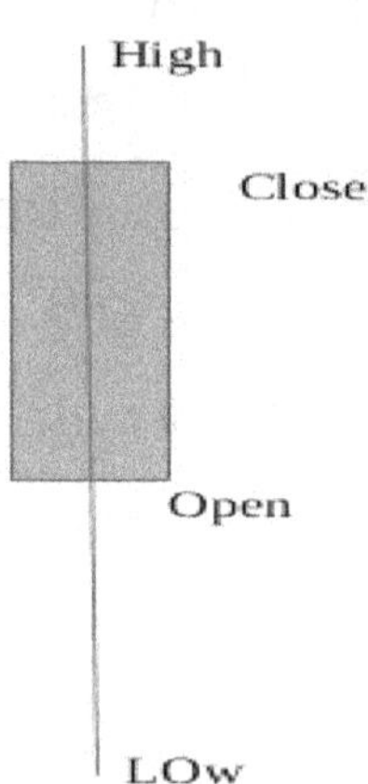

Bearish candle:

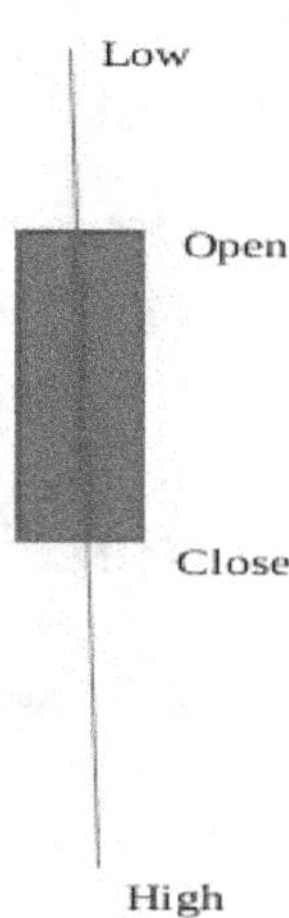

Just like a bar chart, a daily candlestick shows the market's open, high, low, and close price for the day. The candlestick has a wide part, which is called the "real body."

This real body represents the price range between the open and close of that day's trading. When the real body is filled in or black, it means the close was lower than the open. If the real body is empty, it means the close was higher than the open.

Traders can alter these colours in their trading platform. For example, a down candle is often shaded red instead of black, and up candles are often shaded green instead of white

Charts:

Different Types of Charts

Technical analysts use a variety of charts based on the information they seek. However, there are three types of charts that are most commonly used. They are:

Line charts

A line chart is probably the most common type of chart. This chart tracks the closing prices of the stock over a specific period.

Each closing price point is represented by a dot. And all the dots are connected by lines to get the graphical representation.

While it is considered to be quite simplistic (compared to other chart types), a line chart helps traders to spot trends in the price movement. However, since it tracks closing prices, it does not offer much information regarding intraday price movement.

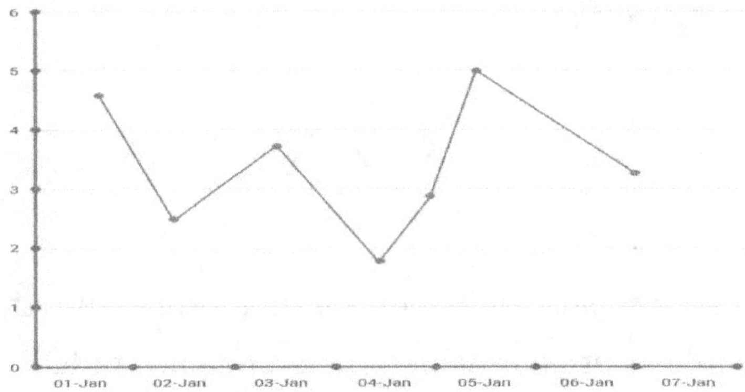

X-axis represents the time period while the Y-axis represents the stock price

Bar charts

A bar chart is quite similar to a line chart. However, it offers much more information. Instead of a dot, each plot point in the graph is represented by a vertical line. This line has two horizontal lines extending from both the sides.

It is represented as follows:

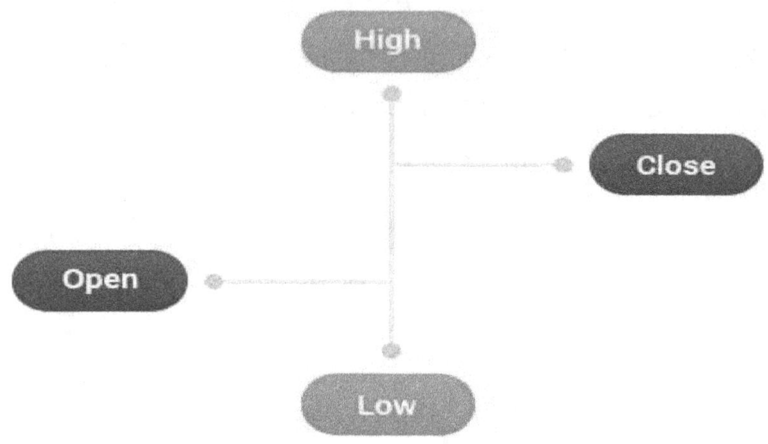

The top part of the vertical line represents the highest price at which the stock had traded during the day.

Similarly, the lower part represents the lowest traded price. The left extension represents the price at which the stock opened while the right extension represents the closing price for the day.

In addition to offering greater detail than a line chart, the bar chart also gives insight on volatility. If the line is longer, it means that there was greater volatility in the trading of the stock.

Candlestick charts

Candlestick charts are very popular among technical analysts. They offer a great deal of information in a very precise manner. As the name suggests, the price movements for each day are represented in the shape of a candlesticks.

It is similar to a bar chart because it represents the four data points: high, low, open and close.

While bar charts give volatile information only for a single trading day, candlestick charts can offer this information for a much larger time period. In addition, the candlesticks come in different colours based on the price movements.

A falling candlestick is generally represented by a black or red body while a rising candlestick is represented by a white or clear body.

Candlestick chart with respect to time frame

1 min time frame chart   5 min time frame

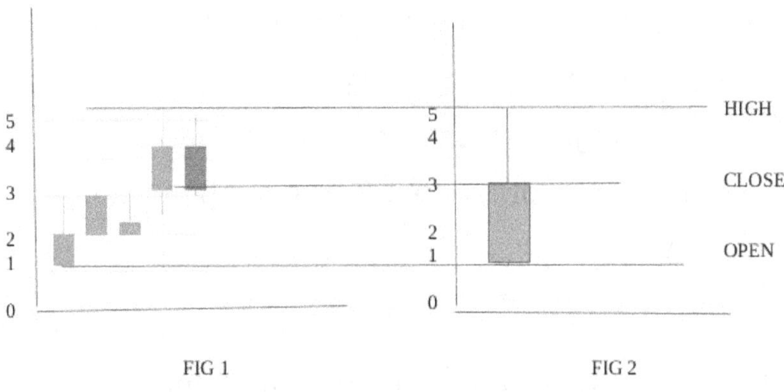

Both (Fig 1 and Fig 2) are related to each other

Trading types:

There are multiple trading types,

Day Trading :

Method of buying and selling securities within the same day, position are closed out within the same day and no position is held overnight.

Swing Trading:

Swing trading is usually held for more than a day but for a shorter time than trend trades, a range-bound is a risk for swing traders

Scalping:

One of the quickest strategies employed by active traders, take advantage of small moves that occur frequently with large size

Position Trading:

Uses longer-term charts anywhere from daily to weekly. In combination with other methods to determine the trend of the current market direction

Volume

Volume is the amount of stock that has been bought and sold within a specific period of time. If a stock moves on low volume, it means that few people are participating in the current price movement and the trend may not continue. Meanwhile, if a stock moves on high volume, it means many people are involved in the trade and the trend is more likely to continue.

Let's say 10 people sold 50,000 **shares** of Company A on a given day then 50k would be the **volume**. Or, X sold 1,000 **shares** to Z and bought back those 1,000 **shares** then the **volume** would be 2k.

Example

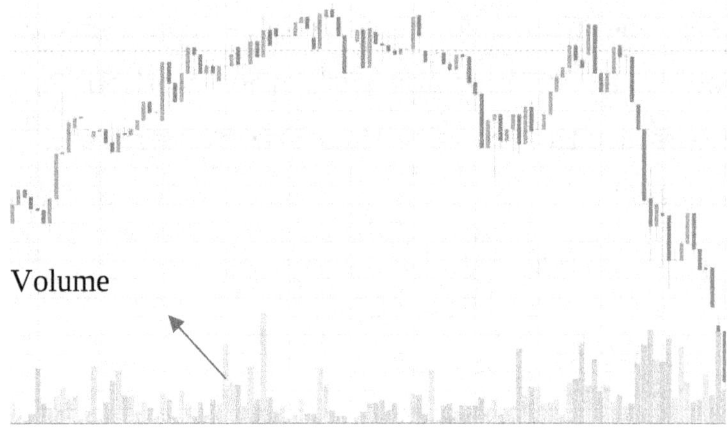

Why you have to trade just like a casino

For anyone who does not know the game, it is called roulette which has 18 black 18 red and 2 green chips.

People may think that when they play this game it is a 50/50 game either you win and double your money or you lose it all.

Let say if you are beating on a number of a colour black we people think it is a 50/50 chance to make it kind of true. If you bet on a number and a colour black you have the probability of winning is 47.3% and for the casino, it is 52.6%, Casino edge over a player is 5.3%

What a casino edge over a player implies is, when a person plays a bet over $1, Casino takes 5.4% of the money

if you bet on black

player => 18/38 = 47.3%

casino=> 20/38 = 52.6%

And in the long run bet casino takes 5.4% of the money and whenever a bet is placed for $1 casino edge is 0.054 and if the bet is the place for $1million casino edge will be $54,000

To break the $54k down,

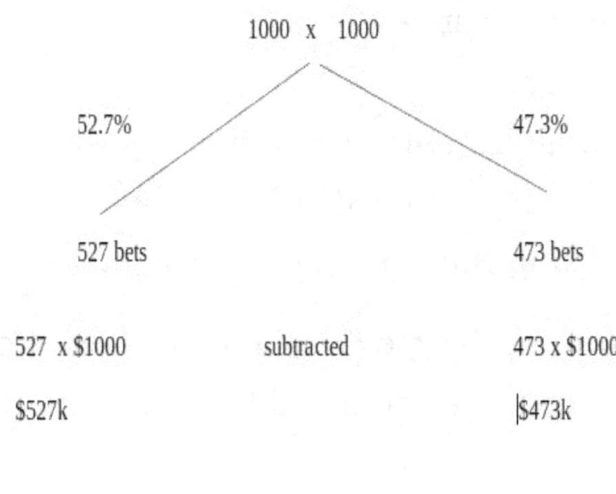

well in the casino's case: it's risk and reward ratio is 1:1

Different Types of Candlesticks

- Big Candles
- Dojis
- Gravestone
- Dragonfly
- Shooting Star
- Hammer
- Morning Doji Star / Evening Doji Star
- Bearish Harami / Bullish Harami
- Engulfing Bullish / Engulfing Bearish

Let's explore each type of candle and how it can help you predict patterns and trends.

Big Candles

Big Candles are self-explanatory since they are large candles with major price differences.

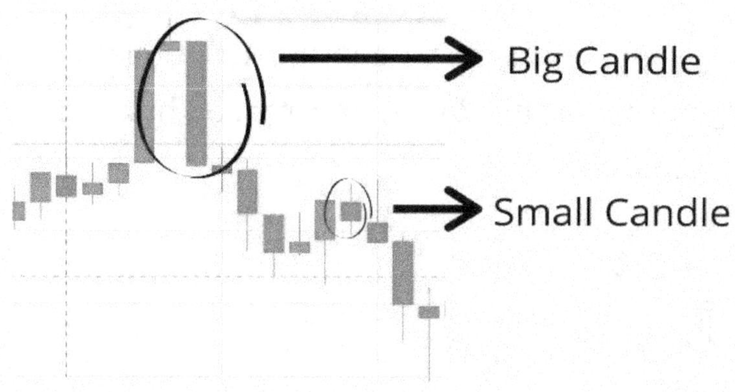

Here is a segment of a candlestick chart that has an example of a big candle compared to a small candle.

The small candle might have been a $0.20 drop-in price where the big candle might have been a $2.00 drop in price. The important thing to note is that big candles are drastic changes in price whether it be increasing or decreasing.

A candle tells us about the current **supply** and **demand** during the lifespan of the candle. A big candlestick that decreases in price means that during that time, supply was much higher than demand. If the candle increases in price, then the demand was higher than supply.

For example, this chart has an exceptionally large drop on this day and is marked by a big red candlestick.

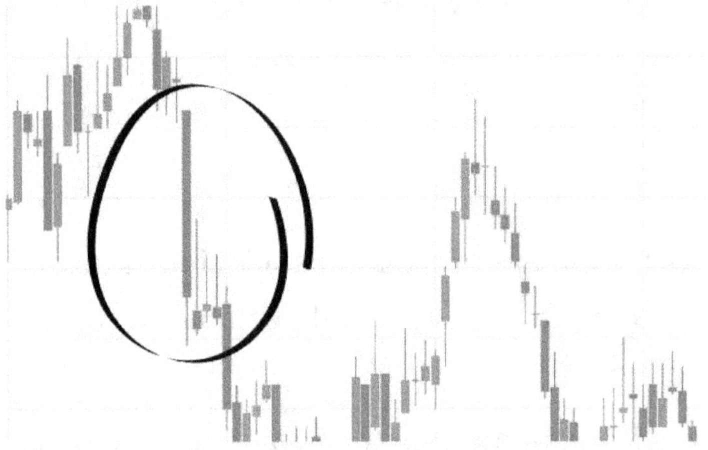

We know right away that supply was much higher than demand on this day- but why such a large drop?

We can assume that there might have been some news or information that caused such a drastic change in price. Let's explore another candlestick form known as a **Doji.**

Dojis

A Doji is a candle that fluctuates in price during a certain period but opens and closes at the same price. The period could be 1 day, 1 hour, or even one minute. The synopsis is still the same- which is that there is **uncertainty in the market**.

At one point, buyers were winning and at one point sellers were winning but it ended up closing at the same price as when it opened. If the candle wick is large, then that simply means that there is higher indecision than a Doji with a small wick.

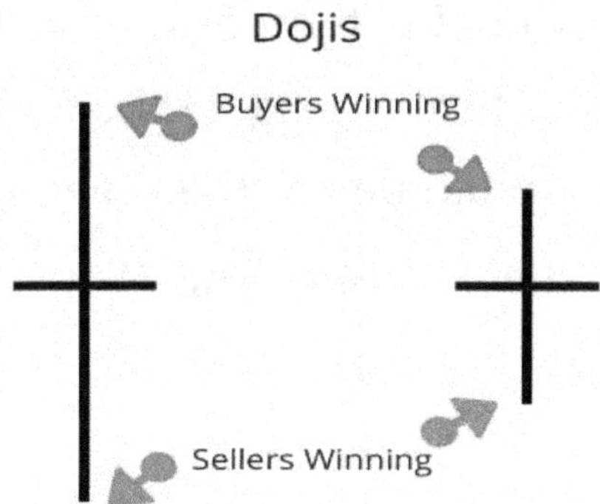

Dojis by themselves tell us that there is indecision on the price but does not tell us much beyond that. Although, if using them with other candlestick patterns, you might be able to learn more about how the stock price is going to move. Two of the patterns are the **morning Doji star** and the **evening Doji star**.

Morning Doji Star and Evening Doji Star

These patterns use the Doji to mark a possible trend reversal. If the candles are moving down and then hit a Doji and begin moving up, this would be an example of the **morning Doji star**. The opposite pattern where the Doji marks a trend reversal going down, then that would be an example of an **evening Doji star**.

Morning Doji Star & Evening Doji Star

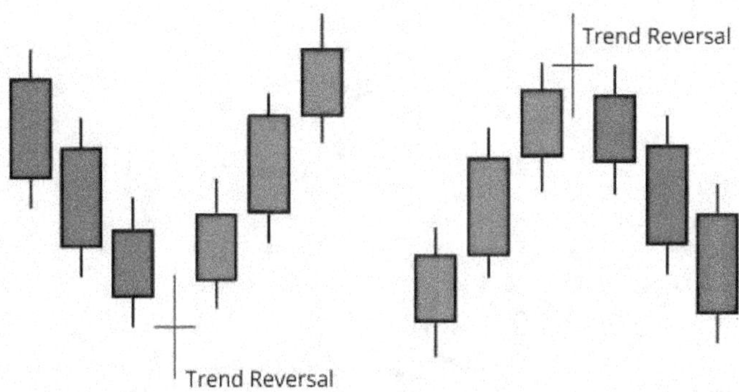

The morning and evening Doji stars are not going to tell you what stocks you should purchase.

You should not simply see this pattern and rush to go purchase.

But, if you have already chosen a stock based on your strategy, this pattern will help tell you the best timing to enter the market.

Also, do not get caught up on searching for a Doji that has an exact match with the opening and closing price. It could also have a small body with similar opening and closing prices.

The point is to have the knowledge of being able to identify the pattern for market entry.

This is an example of a good time to enter the market. The small candle at the bottom is an indicator that the pattern is shifting and there is a trend reversal. It would likely be a good time to purchase after the stock bottomed out and showed promise for growth.

Gravestone and Dragonfly

These two forms of a candle are like the Doji, in that they open and close at the same price, but they only fluctuate in one direction: increasing or decreasing.

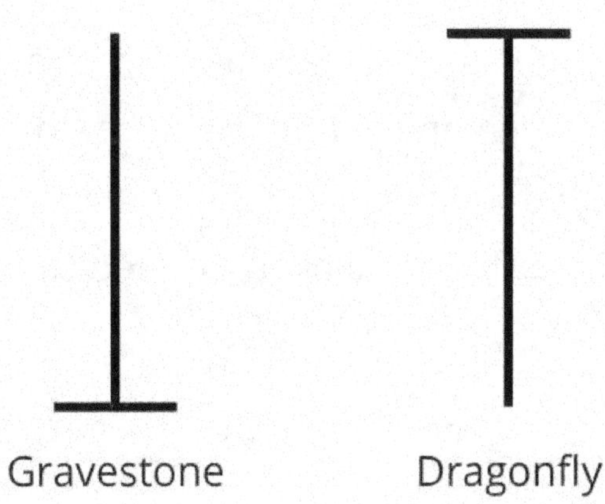

Gravestone   Dragonfly

Similar to the Doji, they will not be very helpful by themselves but using them with other candle forms can help predict the future of a stock.

Shooting Star and Hammer

A **shooting star** is where the stock opens at a price and goes up and then goes down to close just above where it opened. It is almost identical to the **gravestone** but instead closes just above the opening price rather than closing at the same price.

The same goes for the hammer. The **hammer** is where the price opens and the goes down a bit and back up to close just below the opening price. This pattern is closely related to the dragonfly candle type.

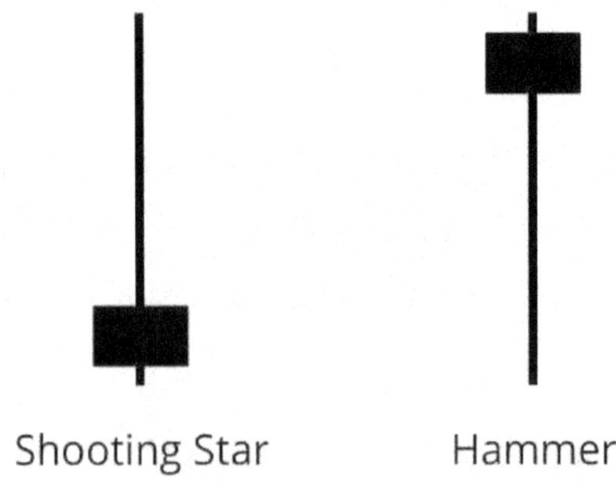

Shooting Star   Hammer

Bearish Harami and Bullish Harami

These patterns consist of a large candle followed by a smaller candle that is contained within the body of the first candle. The **bearish harami** signals a reversal pattern to the downside while the **bullish harami** signals to the upside.

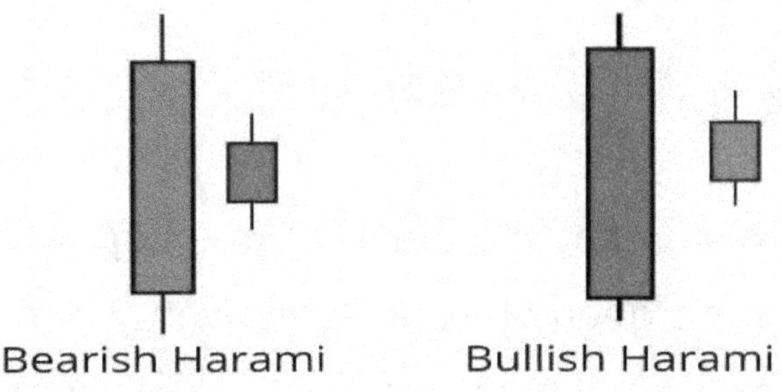

This pattern strongly suggests that the current situation will **reverse**. Let's look at an example of what that might look like on a candlestick chart.

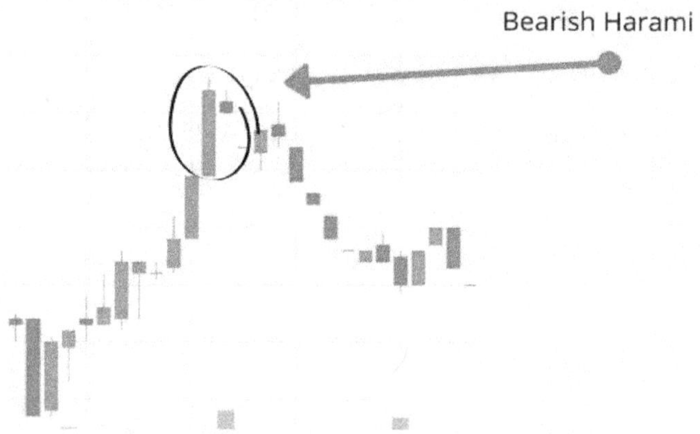

Here we see that the demand was higher than supply for a good streak. The buyers were winning. Then once it reached a certain price, the next opening price was lower and the closing price decreased from there. This is a strong indicator that there is going to be a **trend reversal** and the stock is going to change direction. This tells us that once the stock reached a certain price, it got exhausted and sellers were able to take over the market.

Engulfing Bullish and Engulfing Bearish

This pattern is where a small candlestick is followed by a larger opposite candlestick that fully engulfs the first one.

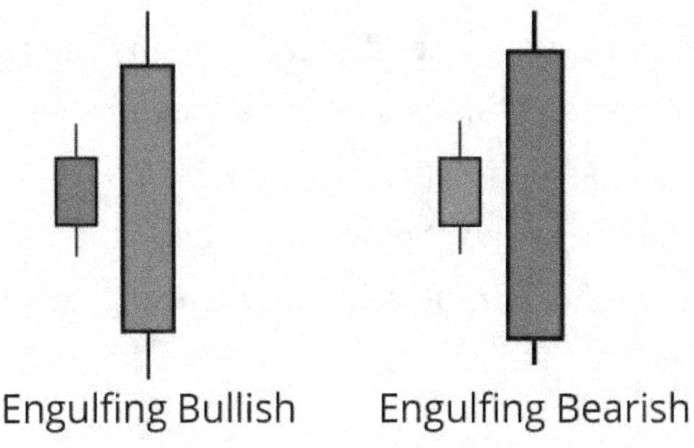

Here is an example of an engulfing bearish pattern.

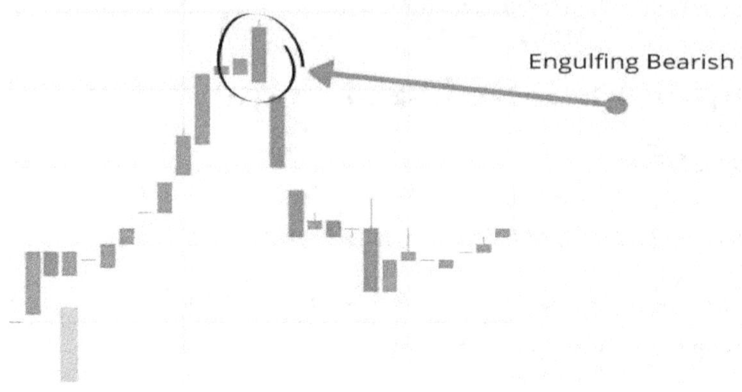

We see that the buyers are buying the driving the price up for some time. Then at the peak, a large red candlestick engulfs the small green candlestick- signalling a trend reversal. This is a strong signal because it tells us that the sellers are overpowering the buyers- and by a lot since it completely engulfs the previous candle.

Are these all the Candlesticks to Know?

There are many more candlesticks that have names attached to them but they are not as important as the ones discussed above. If you spent all of your time memorizing candlestick names and all of the different types, then you would be missing the point.

The goal here is not the name memorization. It is about understanding how certain candles can potentially predict behaviour when placed in a pattern.

What makes prices fluctuate?

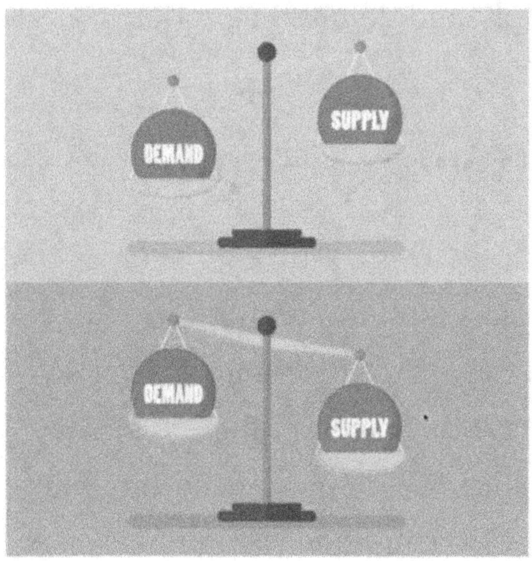

Supply and Demand are the two factors which make the price fluctuate as when there is more supply the demand price goes down and vice versa.

The law of supply and demand is a theory that explains the interaction between the sellers of a resource and the buyers for that resource. The theory defines what effect the relationship between the availability of a particular product and the desire (or demand) for that product has on its price. Generally, low supply and high demand increase price and vice versa. Perfect examples of supply and demand in action include PayPal.

Factors Affecting Supply

Production capacity, production cost such as labour and materials, and the number of competitors directly affect how much supply businesses can create. Ancillary factors such as material availability, weather, and the reliability of supply chains also can affect supply.

Factors Affecting Demand

The number of available substitutes, consumer preferences, and the shifts in the price of complementary products affect demand. For example, if the price of video game consoles drops, the demand for games for that console may increase as more people buy the console and want games for it.

Example:

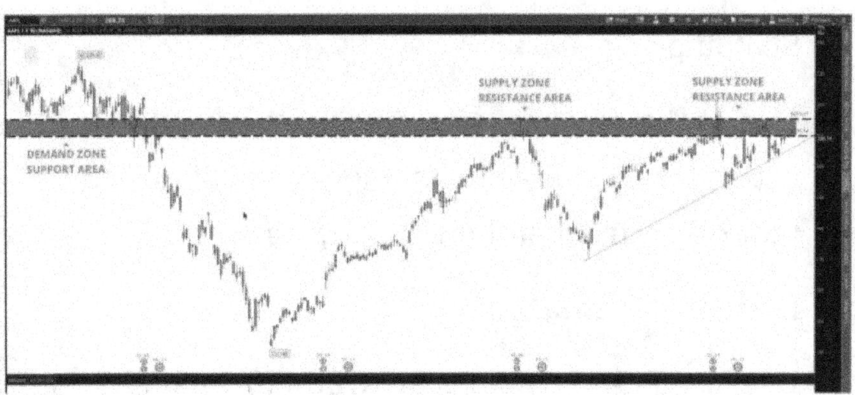

Trading types:

There are multiple trading types,

Day Trading :

Method of buying and selling securities within the same day, position are closed out within the same day and no position is held overnight.

Swing Trading:

Swing trading is usually held for more than a day but for a shorter time than trend trades, a range-bound is a risk for swing traders

Scalping:

One of the quickest strategies employed by active traders, take advantage of small moves that occur frequently with large size

Position Trading:

Uses longer-term charts anywhere from daily to weekly. In combination with other methods to determine the trend of the current market direction

THINGS YOU NEED TO LEARN TO BE A PROFESSIONAL TRADER:

1 . Close stops.

2 . Enter only at the point of least risk.

3 . Study what the market pattern is telling you.

4. Learn the habits of the traders who know what they are doing.

5. Prepare before you sit down to trade.

You have to understand that it does not matter what you think the market will do, it will not go anywhere unless there is an imbalance between the buyers and the sellers. One side needs to be winning for the market to trend.

The other thing is that you can enter the market at any time you get a signal

that is valid. These signals appear 5 or 10 times a day.

Losers never get to learn that the market is easy because they rush in without studying the market flow. Many just listen to brokers and they do not have online data to see what the market is doing.

You have to have the facilities of the professional trader to call yourself one.

Most of all you have to act like one.

The biggest common fault of losers is that they take a position and will not get out of it when the writing is on the wall that they were wrong.

You will always know when you were right and you will always know that if you took a trade and it didn't do what you thought it would you are now wrong. If it looks like it is not working SCRATCH the trade and wait for a better opportunity.

To do anything else is stupidity.

Ask yourself! Would I stay in a high stakes poker game and bet on the next card drawn if I was holding a 7 and an 8 - NO you would just throw them away. Yet if you had a pair of Aces in the hole you would bet the living wits out of the pot.

The first thing you need to learn to be a professional trader is to remove all the stupidity from your game plan. You must have a good reason to take any trade.

One other piece of advice - avoid forecasters as all they will do is cause you to hold losses in the hope the market will come back and save you.

---*The market will never save you - you have to save yourself*---

Decoding the Stock Trading Millionaire's mind:

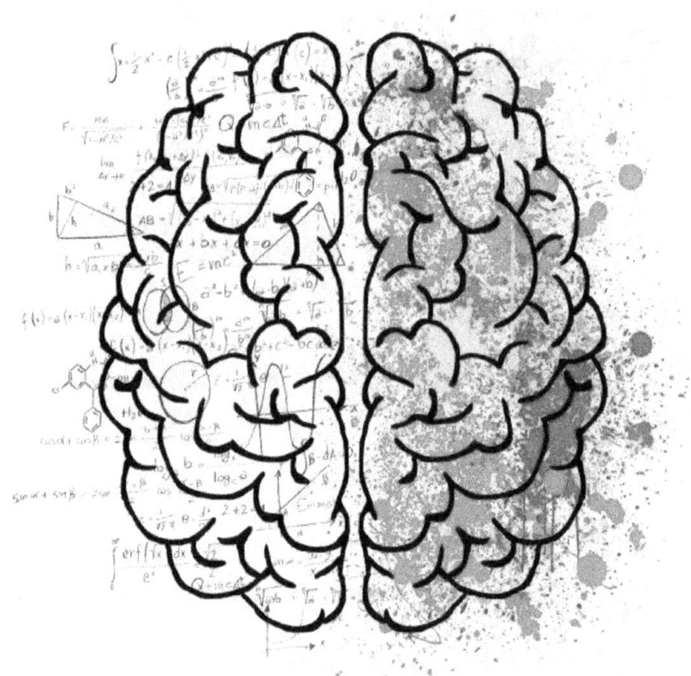

People fail to understand what it is that leads any normal person to become a millionaire by trading stocks. It's not mere "luck," as many would call it, so what is it that has led people to become so successful in the stock market?

The Human Mind.

Millionaire stock traders have several key attributes which are the main cause of their success. Each attribute links to their amazing mindset.

You can provide two people with the exact same information, but the turnout can be completely different, depending on each of their minds.

No one is born with any of these traits, it's definitely something you or anyone else looking to excel can develop.

Number 1: Discipline

The word Discipline is thrown around a lot nowadays.

Of course, everyone knows the general definition which is to train a person to obey rules or a code of behaviour.

While many people do know this, they fail to understand it.

Let me give you an example.

You work for a company that requires you to be at work every morning by 9:00 AM SHARP. No excuses. Your boss is pretty strict about latecomers, so you make sure to be on time, every single day.

So let's say you work 5 days a week, Monday — Friday, 9:00 am to 5:00 pm. You're up every morning by about 7:00 am, and out of the house by 8:00 am. You arrive at the office at 8:45 am just to be on the safe side.

So it seems like you've got a pretty good structure going on, right?

One day you realize that you really want financial freedom, and to begin trading FULL TIME. Your boss sucks, and you read an amazing article about being your OWN boss, cool!

You think to yourself, "If I quit my job I'll find myself more available to trade since I'm already up at 7 am every morning anyways."

So you make the insane decision and finally quit your job. Yay...

This is where things go downhill.

You suddenly find yourself without a boss, without a schedule or even without a specific work structure.

No more waking up at 7 am.

No more being up and on your computer watching the markets by 9 am.

No more... structure.

Instead, you're waking up at 1 pm every day unsure of what to do with your life.

Wait, wait, wait..... What went wrong?

It's simple. You had absolutely no control over yourself. A case that lacks discipline.

Your brain was not wired in a way to follow a code of behaviour, or structure on your own. A job is what provided you, with that structure that you might have falsely perceived as a discipline.

Your brain was not wired in a way to follow a code of behaviour, or structure on your own.

A job is what provided you with that structure that you might have falsely perceived as a discipline.

Those people who are able to acquire a strong level of discipline are able to exceed in the Stock Market and acquire success. In comparison to those who fail to control their negative habits and traits.

You have to develop a strong mental framework that will ensure you will remain motivated and focused regardless of conflicts and mistakes.

Here's how you can develop Self Discipline:

Start off by creating a trading plan, and STICKING TO IT. You need to set clear goals and have an execution plan.

A clear path will outline each step required for you to reach your goals.

When you're trading you probably notice at times when you have a plan outlined and you actually don't follow it.

Now discipline kicks in where you have to get your mind to a place where you are able to follow that plan you are able to execute the trades that you have laid out. If you don't have that discipline you're not going to be able to control yourself when you are in that situation to actually execute certain trades.

A special way to combat losing focus is through meditation. You must understand that we are not born with self-discipline. It is a trait which we, as humans, must learn as a daily practice.

Meditation will strengthen your willpower, which FUELS success.

Try it out. See how it goes, and remember to stay consistent.

Consistency plays a large role in developing discipline, which brings us into the second attribute which every Stock trading millionaire has acquired.

Number 2: Consistency.

It will ultimately help you in the long run by allowing you to build strong habits to succeed.

Think about it for a second.

A surgeon, to us, seems like a very sophisticated and high-end job. For those who are not surgeons, it's impossible for us to do their job. But for a skilled surgeon, it's nothing more than a routine which has been executed hundreds of times.

Brain surgery? No biggie.

It's the same case for any successful trader. It seems like this high-end professional career that an outsider would know absolutely nothing about. But what people don't realize is that both surgeons and stock traders, (as well as many other professional fields) have a consistent pattern in their procedures.

Consistency builds Habit.

Sticking to an effective trading method, or trading plan will provide you with the chance to succeed in the market. And even if you don't succeed right away, you'll be able to learn from your mistakes and keep going.

Switching between different methods or different styles will hurt you in the long run, and hold you back. Is that what you want?

No? I thought so. So stay consistent!

Here's how you can develop consistency:

I've learned from a lot of people that it's really difficult for them to remain consistent on just about anything. It definitely is much more difficult than it seems, but it isn't impossible.

Start off by setting some realistic goals for yourself to understand what you want, and why you want it. Get a proper understanding of what your life would be like if you picked up this habit.

For instance, when I was first getting started in trading, I had a board in my room with images of everything I was working for. It included my family, a home, a car, and overall a better lifestyle. Every morning when I woke up I was reminded of my goals and it motivated me.

Next, I had a schedule of how my day should be going and what I had to do at specific times. It kept me on track and made sure that I wasn't slacking on ANY task.

Write out your goals, remind yourself of them every morning, follow your schedule, and build POSITIVE habits.

If you want to drink more water, set an appointment on your calendar to chime once every two hours telling you to go drink a cup of water.

If you want to meditate every morning at 7:00 am, set an alarm to remind you.

Putting everything on your calendar or writing it down provides it with much more importance than by keeping it in your head.

Trust me, you're going to forget. Write it down.

Get back up, and KEEP GOING.

Let's face it. Building habits isn't easy. You probably won't stay consistent the first time you give it a go. No matter what level of commitment we have or even how strong our why is, we're human. Stuff happens.

Accept that you failed, and just try again.

Number 3: Accountability.

Accountability is not stressed enough in the markets but will accelerate your performance, BIG TIME.

When working a 9–5 job, people are automatically held accountable for their actions considering they have someone constantly watching over them. That's how things are always running smoothly in any successful business.

But what happens when there's no one there to hold you accountable?

Most successful people have already come to the conclusion that when they are held accountable only to themselves, it does not prove to be as efficient. It's easier to give up when no one's there to make sure you're on track.

But don't worry... I have a solution for you.

All you have to do is team up with someone; a fellow trader, a friend, a family member, or anyone who you feel would be able to positively impact you in this matter. We'll call this person your accountability coach.

Not only will an accountability coach boost performance, but it will also help you measure success and progress.

Your subconscious mind will be aware that you have to track and report your results to another person which will help you remain focused. You'll be encouraged to set goals for yourself and achieve them, making this whole thing a positive experience.

There are many trading group-chats out there that will allow you to meet new people who would be thrilled to become a part of your journey. Each of you can hold one another accountable for the goals you set, and to ensure you're both always on track.

So, what are you waiting for? Find your accountability coach now.

Number 4: Passion.

Do you need passion in order to succeed as a trader?

My answer is yes.

Overall, anyone who is passionate about what they do will be both happier and more productive in their career. The many extraordinary individuals who have become millionaires through stock trading are personally invested in and motivated by its mission.

"Choose a job you love, and you will never have to work a day in your life,"

– Confucius

Passion is one of the most controversial attributes, as many people tend to disagree with it. Mark Cuban, believes one of the greatest lies in life is to follow your passion. But I believe otherwise.

What most people can agree on, is that enjoying your career path in life is difficult to fake. Either you feel it, or you don't. You spend most of your daily hours working, and if you are not passionate about what you do the entire day, then I doubt you'll secure the results that you desire.

If you want to taste the flavour of success, you have to be passionate about whatever it is that you're doing. If you want to trade simply to make money, I suggest you find another career path. Passion will help you to develop a growth mindset, intensify focus, enable creativity & innovation, and enhance your desire to Pursue EXCELLENCE.

Trade with passion, and watch your results excel. Trading without passion will just lead you to become uninterested the moment you make a mistake.

Overall structure to make a trade

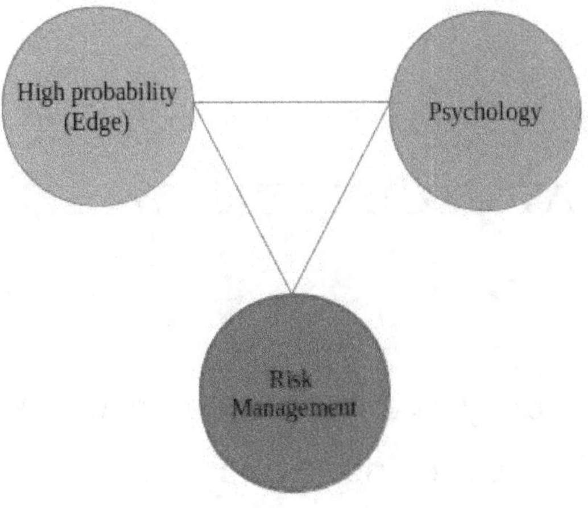

Combining them with your trading style make you a profitable and consistent trader

So why do the people fail in the Market?

After having a heck of knowledge in Trading why people fail is they lack either one of the structures in their trading system which makes them have a huge fat loss in their account.

ATTITUDE SURVEY

1. To make money as a trader you have to know what the market is going to do next.

Agree Disagree

2. Sometimes I find myself thinking that there must be a way to trade without having to take a loss.

Agree Disagree

3. Making money as a trader is primarily a function of analysis.

Agree Disagree

4. Losses are an unavoidable component of trading.

Agree Disagree

5. My risk is always defined before I enter a trade.

Agree Disagree

6. In my mind, there is always a cost associated with finding out what the market may do next.

Agree Disagree

7. I wouldn't even bother putting on the next trade if I wasn't sure that it was going to be a winner.

Agree Disagree

8. The more a trader learns about the markets and how they behave, the easier it will be for him to execute his trades.

Agree Disagree

9. My methodology tells me exactly under what market conditions to either enter or exit a trade.

Agree Disagree

10. Even when I have a clear signal to reverse my position, I find it extremely difficult to do.

Agree Disagree

11. I have sustained periods of consistent success usually followed by some fairly drastic draw-downs in my equity.

Agree Disagree

12. When I first started trading I would describe my trading methodology as haphazard, meaning some success in between a lot of pain.

Agree Disagree

13. I often find myself feeling that the markets are against me personally.

Agree Disagree

14. As much as I might try to "let go," I find it very difficult to put past emotional wounds behind me.

Agree Disagree

15. I have a money management philosophy that is founded in the principle of always taking some money out of the market when the market makes it available.

Agree Disagree

16. A trader's job is to identify patterns in the markets' behaviour that represent an opportunity and then to determine the risk of finding out if these patterns will play themselves out as they have in the past.

Agree Disagree

17. Sometimes I just can't help feeling that I am a victim of the market.

Agree Disagree

18. When I trade I usually try to stay focused in a one-time frame.

Agree Disagree

19. Trading successfully requires a degree of mental flexibility far beyond the scope of most people.

Agree Disagree

20. There are times when I can definitely feel the flow of the market; however, I often have difficulty acting on these feelings.

Agree Disagree

21. There are many times when I am in a profitable trade and I know the move is basically over, but I still won't take my profits.

Agree Disagree

22. No matter how much money I make in a trade, I am rarely ever satisfied and feel that I could have made more.

Agree Disagree

23. When I put on a trade, I feel I have a positive attitude. I anticipate all of the money I could make from the trade in a positive way.

Agree Disagree

24. The most important component in a trader's ability to accumulate money over time is having a belief in his own consistency.

Agree Disagree

25. If you were granted a wish to be able to instantaneously acquire one trading skill, what skill would

you choose?

26. I often spend sleepless nights worrying about the market.

Agree Disagree

27. Do you ever feel compelled to make a trade because you are afraid that you might miss out?

Yes No

28. Although it doesn't happen very often, I really like my trades to be perfect. When I make a perfect call it feels so good that it makes up for all of the times that I don't.

Agree Disagree

29. Do you ever find yourself planning trades you never execute, and executing trades you never planned?

Yes No

30. In a few sentences explain why most traders either don't make money or aren't able to keep what they make.

WHY THIS BOOK ?

Do you alienate your self from the stock market just because of the fear of not making it? Worry not! You have got plenty to pocket once you start making the right decisions with precision and technique. Do not back off even before getting a taste of marking your first step on the rubble road (It could become a piece of cake once you master it). If you're looking for a book that can make your path easier and guide you towards the lane of success, this is the book for you. Help yourself overcome that very fear of not making it and reach your pinnacle of power in no time at all! So, why wait when there is everything you would possibly need right in your hands? Stop worrying about making it big and start worrying about precision and you're good to go. Start your journey today and become a stock market Genius

For any queries you can reach me through my mail (adi2132000@gmail.com)